What Does the Mayor Do?

UNDERSTANDING GOVERNMENT

Sadie Silva

CIVICS FOR THE REAL WORLD™

Rosen Classroom™

What does the mayor do?

The mayor runs the city!

The mayor works at city hall. City hall is a big building downtown.

The mayor talks to many people. She wants to help make the city better.

The mayor listens to what the people want. She helps plan a new park.

The mayor helps make new laws for the city. We can ride bikes here now.

The mayor keeps the city running smoothly. Many people help her.

The mayor gets things done.
She has people fix the roads.

The mayor works with police. She wants to keep the city safe.

People vote for the mayor. They pick the person who will do the best job.

The mayor works hard for the city.
Could you be the mayor someday?

WORDS TO KNOW

bike

city hall